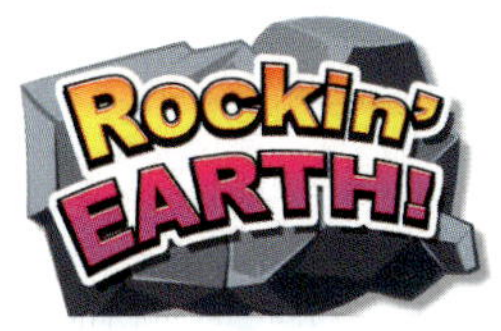

MAGNIFICENT METAMORPHIC ROCK

by Rex Ruby

Minneapolis, Minnesota

Credits

Cover and title page, © Angus Mackie/Alamy Stock Photo; 4–5 © Chansak Joe/iStock; 6, © eagledwarf/Adobe Stock; 7, © robertcicchetti/iStock; 8L, © vvoe/Adobe Stock; 8R, © VvoeVale/iStock; 9T, © Peter Cripps/Adobe Stock; 9M, © VisualMarketplace/Adobe Stock; 9B, © fotogurmespb/Adobe Stock; 10, © HRAUN/iStock; 11, © Shutterstock; 13, © Shutterstock; 14–15, © Les Palenik/Adobe Stock; 16–17, © Vladone/iStock; 18, © Massimo Santi/Shutterstock; 19, © U.S. National Archives and Records Administration/Wikimedia Commons; 20, © Paolo Gagliardi/iStock; 21T, © Alan Morris/iStock; 21B, © Vyshedko/Shutterstock; 22, © FatCamera/iStock and © Kansitang P/Shutterstock; Used Throughout, © vaitekune/Adobe Stock and © Dmytro Synelnychenko/iStock.

Bearport Publishing Company Product Development Team

President: Jen Jenson; Director of Product Development: Spencer Brinker; Managing Editor: Allison Juda; Associate Editor: Naomi Reich; Associate Editor: Tiana Tran; Art Director: Colin O'Dea; Designer: Kim Jones; Designer: Kayla Eggert; Product Development Assistant: Owen Hamlin

STATEMENT ON USAGE OF GENERATIVE ARTIFICIAL INTELLIGENCE

Bearport Publishing remains committed to publishing high-quality nonfiction books. Therefore, we restrict the use of generative AI to ensure accuracy of all text and visual components pertaining to a book's subject. See BearportPublishing.com for details.

A NOTE FROM THE PUBLISHER:

Some of the historic photos in this book have been colorized to help readers have a more meaningful and rich experience. The color results are not intended to depict actual historical detail.

Library of Congress Cataloging-in-Publication Data is available at www.loc.gov or upon request from the publisher.

ISBN: 979-8-89232-029-0 (hardcover)
ISBN: 979-8-89232-506-6 (paperback)
ISBN: 979-8-89232-158-7 (ebook)

For more information, write to Bearport Publishing, 5357 Penn Avenue South, Minneapolis, MN 55419.

CONTENTS

A STATUE MADE FROM ROCK

Each year, millions of people visit a huge statue of President Abraham Lincoln in Washington, D.C. The figure is so shiny and smooth, it may be hard to believe that it's carved out of rock. **Sculptors** made the statue from marble. Where does this impressive rock come from, and how does it form?

The marble statue is called the Lincoln Memorial. It is 19 feet (6 m) tall.

The Lincoln Memorial is in an area known as the National Mall.

METAMORPHIC ROCK

Marble is a type of **metamorphic** (*met*-uh-MOR-fik) rock. Like all metamorphic rocks, it starts as another kind of rock. This original rock, called a parent rock, gets put under high **pressure**, extremely high **temperatures**, or both. The shift to something new is actually how the rock gets its name. *Metamorphic* comes from a Greek word that means change in form.

Metamorphic rock forms underground, deep within Earth.

CHANGING ROCK

Which rocks change into metamorphic rocks? Scientists sort rocks into three main types. In addition to metamorphic rocks, there are **sedimentary** (*sed*-uh-MEN-tuhree) and **igneous** (IG-nee-uhs) rocks. Both igneous and sedimentary rocks can turn into metamorphic rocks. Marble starts as a sedimentary rock called limestone. Granite (GRAN-it) is an igneous rock that changes into gneiss (NISE), another metamorphic rock.

Igneous rock
Metamorphic rock
Sedimentary rock

INSIDE EARTH'S CRUST

The changes that create metamorphic rock happen deep underground inside Earth's **crust.** This rocky layer of the planet is made up of many different types of rocks, including igneous and sedimentary rocks. A superhot melted rock called **magma** flows in a liquid form just beneath the crust. Heat from magma can change the rock to a metamorphic one.

Magma that flows onto Earth's surface is called lava.

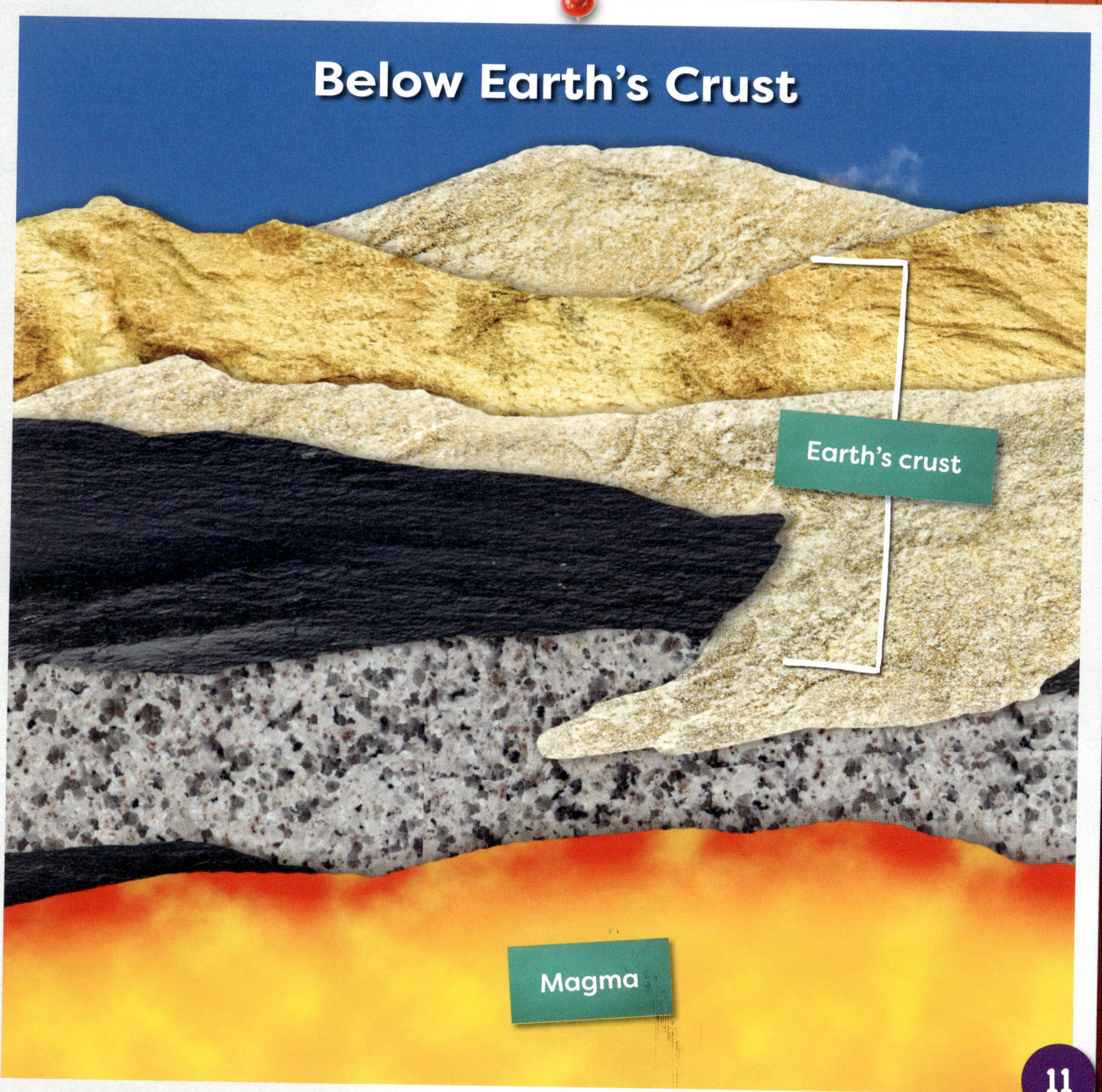
Below Earth's Crust
Earth's crust
Magma

BAKING NEW ROCK

When a crack forms in Earth's crust, magma oozes into the space. The rocks around the magma start to heat up. They bake into metamorphic rock. If limestone is around the crack, the metamorphic rock formed is marble. This process of heating the parent rock into metamorphic rock can take thousands of years.

Too much heat can melt the rock. When this superhot liquid rock cools, it forms igneous rock.

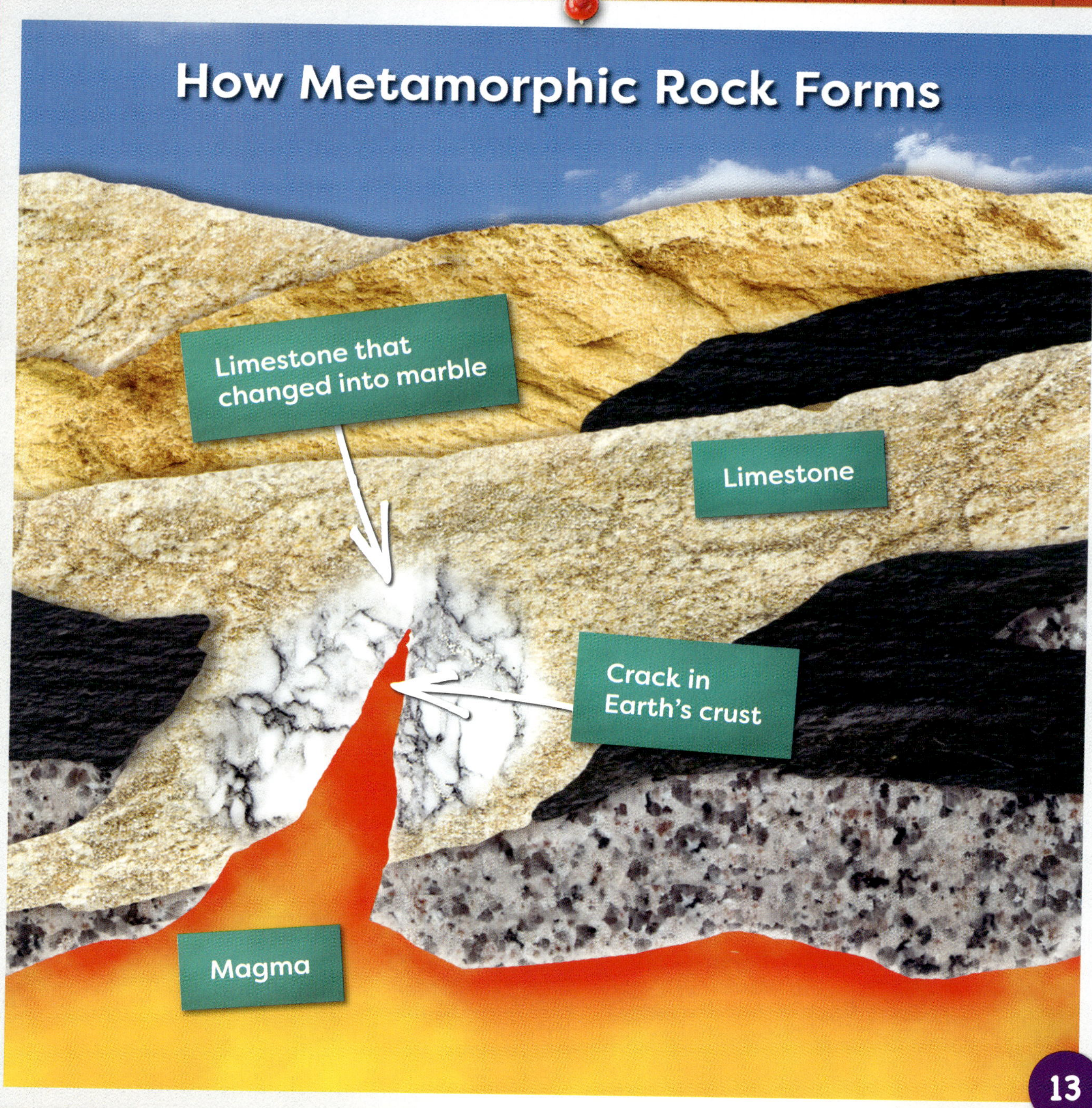
How Metamorphic Rock Forms
Limestone that changed into marble
Limestone
Crack in Earth's crust
Magma

CRUSHING

Heat from magma is not the only thing that can form metamorphic rock. Sometimes, cracks in Earth's crust can cause the crust to move. As it shifts, rocks are crushed, stretched, and folded against one another. These movements create lots of pressure, which can also turn rocks into metamorphic rocks.

The swirled patterns on some metamorphic rocks show where the parent rock was folded and stretched.

Folds in gneiss

FINDING ROCKS

Since metamorphic rocks form deep underground, how do people find and use these rocks for things like statues? Sometimes, wind and rain wear away rock on Earth's surface. This causes the top layers of soft rock to crumble and break up. Then, they get washed or blown away. Over time, the underground metamorphic rock gets uncovered.

Some metamorphic rocks are pushed to the surface as Earth's crust cracks and moves.

A rock that has been worn away
to leave behind metamorphic rock

MARBLE FOR A STATUE

In **quarries**, people dig into the earth to get to buried rock. Quarry workers cut metamorphic rocks from mountainsides or from the ground. About 100 years ago, marble for Lincoln's statue was cut from a quarry in Georgia. What started as 28 blocks of marble were carved into the famous president.

A marble quarry

Sculptors carved Lincoln's statue in pieces and then put them together.

CHECK OUT SOME ROCKS

Metamorphic rocks are always forming. Baking and crushing changes parent sedimentary and igneous rocks into metamorphic rocks. Even metamorphic rocks can become new ones with the right pressure or heat! Old rocks are always changing into new rocks deep below our feet.

The people that study rocks are called **geologists**.

Phyllite

Slate

Phyllite (FYE-lite) is a metamorphic rock that started as slate (slayt), a different metamorphic rock.

SCIENCE LAB

Make Metamorphic Rock

Using modeling clay, show how metamorphic rocks form from other rocks.

1. Use colored clay to make a model of sedimentary rock. Stack many colors together so you can see layers of rock.

Sedimentary rock

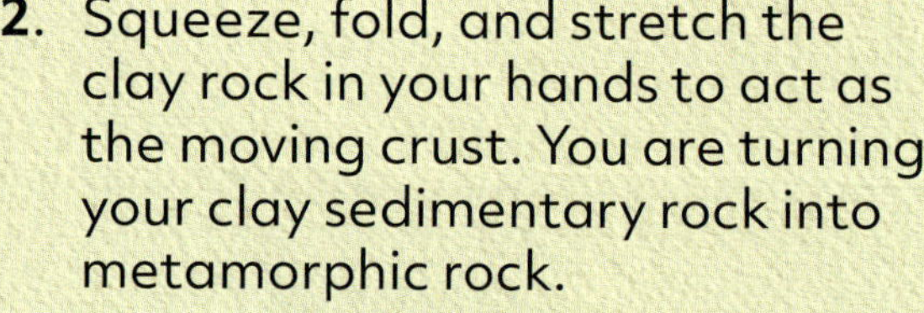

2. Squeeze, fold, and stretch the clay rock in your hands to act as the moving crust. You are turning your clay sedimentary rock into metamorphic rock.

Metamorphic rock

Your clay sedimentary rock still has the same ingredients. But by crushing it, you've changed it into a new kind of metamorphic rock!

GLOSSARY

crust the hard outer layer of Earth

geologists scientists who study Earth's rocks

igneous rock that forms from lava or magma that has cooled and become solid

magma superhot liquid rock found deep inside Earth

metamorphic rock that forms when put under high heat or pressure

pressure the force made by pushing down or pressing on something

quarries places in the ground or along the sides of hills where rock, such as marble or granite, is cut

sculptors artists who use tools to carve or shape statues

sedimentary rock that forms from layers of tiny pieces of rock

temperatures how hot or cold things are

INDEX

READ MORE

McDougal, Anna. *Metamorphic Rocks (Earth's Rocks in Review).* Buffalo, NY: Enslow Publishing, 2024.

Vonder Brink, Tracy. *Metamorphic Rocks (Understanding Geology).* Coral Springs, FL: Seahorse Publishing, 2023.

LEARN MORE ONLINE

1. Go to **www.factsurfer.com** or scan the QR code below.
2. Enter "**Rockin Metamorphic**" into the search box.
3. Click on the cover of this book to see a list of websites.

ABOUT THE AUTHOR

Rex Ruby lives in Minnesota with his family. He likes going on long walks and discovering new rocks along the trail.